GRAEME PO

The Canadian Rockies
A History in Photographs

Altitude Publishing
Canadian Rockies/Vancouver

Above: Byron Harmon with movie camera on Burgess Pass, 1917.

Front Cover: Teepee at Mt. Assiniboine, 1920.

Title Page: Gazebo by the lakeside trail, Lake Louise, ca. 1900.

Back Cover: Captain Conrad O'Brien-ffrench with grizzly bear, ca. 1950.

Copyright © 1991
Altitude Publishing Canada Ltd.

Second, revised edition 1992
Third, revised edition 1993
9 8 7

Made in Western Canada
Printed and bound in Western Canada by Friesen Printers, Altona, Manitoba

Altitude GreenTree Program
Altitude will plant in western Canada twice as many trees as were used in the manufacturing of this book.

Canadian Cataloguing in Publication Data
Pole, Graeme, 1956-
The Canadian Rockies:
A History in Photographs
ISBN 1-55153-900-4
1. Rocky Mountains,
Canadian (B.C. and Alta.) -
History - Pictorial works.*
I. Title.
FC219.P64 1991
971.1'0022'2
C91-091280-7
F1090.p64 1991

Altitude Publishing Canada Ltd. gratefully acknowledges the support of the Canada/Alberta Agreement on the cultural industries.

Design: Robert MacDonald, MediaClones Inc.

Altitude Publishing Canada Ltd.

The Canadian Rockies
1500 Railway Avenue
Canmore, Alberta Canada T1W 1P6

CONTENTS

RAILS INTO THE WILD

Native peoples were the first to see the Canadian Rockies. There is evidence to indicate they traveled, hunted and lived here at least 11,000 years ago. By contrast, the white man's history in the Rockies began in 1754, when fur trader Anthony Henday glimpsed the eastern wall of what he called "The Shining Mountains", from near Innisfail, Alberta. The fur traders eventually established a handful of arduous routes across the Rockies, and a few notable scientists, adventurers, missionaries and explorers added to the knowledge of the land with their travels during the early and mid 1800's. But it was the contact between man and mountains during construction of the Canadian Pacific Railway in the 1880's, which brought the Rockies into the limelight. In the space of less than a decade the railway transformed the mountainous wilds of western Canada from a virtual blank on the map, to a world famous destination.

Canada was only four years old when the idea of a transcontinental railway was first proposed. As part of the deal to lure the resource-rich territory of British Columbia into the country in 1871, Prime Minister John A. Macdonald promised a railway link to the eastern provinces. The same summer, survey crews were dispatched to begin locating a line for the rails across the vast breadth and unknown terrain of central and western Canada; surely one of the most formidable surveying projects ever undertaken.

From proposal to completion, the Canadian Pacific Railway (CPR), as it officially became known, required more than fourteen years. In the end it fell to a syndicate of wealthy businessmen to finance and re-finance the venture. The actual construction occupied four and a half years, and required the efforts of 30,000 workers. The scandal, debate and financial strain of the troubled enterprise brought the young country to the political and financial edge numerous times. Not the least of the challenges to be met in the final survey and construction of the railway, was the first of six great mountain ranges which rose as impenetrable barriers to westward travel into British Columbia, and the dream of uniting Canada by rail – the Canadian Rockies.

Opposite: CPR train alongside the Kicking Horse River, n.d.

Thus, our pictorial history of the Rockies begins in 1882, as the end of railway steel approached the apparent chaos of peaks, valleys, lakes and glaciers, across which the existence of a viable route for the railway had yet to be proven.

The man given the daunting task of finding a route for the CPR through the Rockies, and the unknown Selkirk Mountains further west, was Major A.B. Rogers, an accomplished railway engineer from the United States. With an outlandish moustache, a profane vocabulary, a diet of raw beans and chewing tobacco, and unstoppable drive, "Hell's Bells" Rogers was one of the most colourful characters to grace the pages of Rockies' history. He was from all reports, almost as tough as the mountain landscape he faced in his work.

Rogers drove himself and his men mercilessly hard, earning from most he supervised a respect born out of fear. But if success was the measure of his actions,

Rogers was the right man for the job. He located an acceptable, if hazardous, line for the railway across Kicking Horse and Rogers passes in 1882. For his discovery of Rogers Pass in the Selkirks – the key to the route – the CPR awarded him a 5000 dollar bonus cheque, which Rogers framed and never cashed. Not indestructible, Rogers died from injuries sustained in a fall from his horse in 1889, while surveying another railway in the US.

One of the men in Major Rogers' command was Tom Wilson, who packed supplies for the survey. In August 1882, Wilson was camped with some Stoney Natives at the confluence of the Bow and Pipestone Rivers, near the present site of Lake Louise village.

Wilson heard the thunder of avalanches coming from the mountains above, and asked one of the Natives the source of the sound. He replied the avalanches were on "snow mountain above the lake of little fishes." Next day, Wilson and the Stoney, Edwin Hunter, rode to the lake. Originally named "Emerald" by Wilson, this was the first recorded visit to what is now known as Lake Louise. It also marked the beginning of the connection between the CPR and the spectacular scenery of the Rockies; a connection which would lead to the establishment of a mountain tourism industry and Canada's first three national parks.

Tom Wilson became a fixture in the Canadian Rockies, and something of a

living legend. His extensive knowledge of the landscape almost guaranteed success in mountaineering and hunting ventures, and his services were sought by many at the turn of the century.

Turning Major Rogers' surveyed line through the mountains into rails of steel was a formidable and dangerous task. On the prairies, with little in the way of obstacles, railway work gangs sometimes

Opposite. C.P.R construction gang on the Big Hill, Mt. Stephen in the background, 1884.

Top. Tom Wilson on the shore of Lake Louise in 1930, 48 years after its discovery.

Right. Major A.B. "Hell's Bells" Rogers, surveyor of the route for the C.P.R.in the Rockies and Selkirks.

Turning Major Rogers' surveyed line through the mountains into rails of steel was a formidable and dangerous task. On the prairies, with little in the way of obstacles, railway work gangs sometimes managed to lay more than six miles of track a day. After crossing the Continental Divide, progress slowed, as the workers toiled on hazardous sideslopes above the narrow canyon of the Kicking Horse River, threatened by rockfall, avalanche, and the hazards of working with dynamite. The workers overcame these dangers, and the tracks crossed the Rockies to Golden, British Columbia in 1884.

During construction of the CPR, the "end of steel" was the place to be. For a time in 1883, the steel stopped at Silver City, in the Bow Valley near Castle Mountain. Here, a railway boom town flourished, with the rumoured presence of silver thrown in to heighten the rush. At its peak, Silver City boasted half a dozen hotels and a population larger than Calgary's. When the rails moved west and the silver proved nonexistent, Silver City quickly went from boom to bust. Except for one die-hard resident, it lay deserted two years later. Today, all that remains is a cleared meadow beside the Bow Valley Parkway.

Above: Silver City, railway and mining boom town of 1883-85.

Opposite top: The railway siding of Laggan in 1885. The siding name was changed to Lake Louise in 1913.

Opposite bottom: CPR section gang on a hand car, 1887 or 1888.

The origin of the CPR's mountain hotels has a stronger connection to the logistics and economics of railway operation, than any original desire to establish a business in tourism. To save the expense of hauling heavy dining cars up and down the grades of Kicking Horse and Rogers passes, the CPR constructed Mt. Stephen House at Field in 1886, and stationed a dining car at Rogers Pass, replacing it with a building called Glacier House a year later. Passengers could step off the train and dine in the heart of a fantastic mountain landscape, which four years earlier had been uninhabited, trackless bush. It was an experience unique in the world of travel.

The dining facilities were the brainchild of William Cornelius Van Horne, appointed General Manager of the CPR in 1881, and later its Vice-President. With a successful railway record in the US, Van Horne was touted as "the ablest railway general in the world", and was brought to Canada to oversee the construction and operation of the CPR. Given the huge debt incurred in construction of the railway, Van Horne was always on the lookout for ways to save and make money in the railway's operations. In this he was very successful.

When he saw the popularity of the dining stops, he quickly expanded facilities to allow overnight accommodation. A fledgling railway, the CPR found itself in the hotel business as well.

Along with his business acumen and managerial skill, the dynamic Van Horne is best remembered for his strong advocacy of national parks. It was largely as a result of his lobbying that Banff, Yoho and Glacier national parks came into being in 1885 and 1886. Van Horne's name is commemorated in the range of mountains immediately west of Field.

Opposite: CPR locomotive 314 at Field. This locomotive had a gruesome history. One worker died when it "ran away" on the Big Hill. The engine was repaired, and exploded six years later while going up the hill, killing three.

Top: Mt. Stephen House and the station platform at Field, 1898.

Right: William Cornelius Van Horne, Vice-President and General Manager of the Canadian Pacific Railway.

Operation of the CPR on the treacherous Big Hill near Field, proved a costly and dangerous undertaking. Runaway trains can occur on hills steeper than 1%. The railway's contract with the federal government permitted a maximum grade of 2.2%, yet the grade surveyed on the Big Hill was twice that. Despite the obvious dangers, Van Horne chose a "temporary solution", and ran the rails straight down the hill. He planned to rectify the problem when the CPR was in a better financial position.

Opposite: CPR train in the portal of the lower Spiral Tunnel, n.d.

Top: Open-air observation car at Lake Louise station, 1927.

The first construction train to attempt descent of the Big Hill, ran away and plunged into the canyon, killing three workers. A system of manual safety switches was subsequently installed. Manned around the clock, these switches diverted runaway trains onto spur lines. Train size and speed were restricted, but still the runaways and wrecks occurred. Uphill trains fared little better. Some locomotives exploded under the stress. The steep grade required four locomotives to haul a 15 car train, and additional "pusher" locomotives were sometimes dispatched from Field to help trains stalled on the hill.

The problems posed by Van Horne's "temporary solution" were finally rectified in 1909 with the completion of the ingenious Spiral Tunnels. These two tunnels combine to create a figure eight deep within Mt. Ogden and Cathedral Mountain, adding nearly 7 kilometres to the length of the line, and reducing the overall grade to 2.2 per cent. Two years, 1000 men and almost 700,000 kilograms of dynamite were required in the tunnels' construction.

Main Street and Cascade Mountain, 9,796 ft. Banff, Canadian Rockies.

THE COMFORTS OF HOME

The histories of the Canadian Pacific Railway, Canada's national park system, and the town of Banff are inextricably entwined in a remarkable fabric of endeavour, circumstance and discovery. In November 1883, as construction of the CPR in the Bow Valley wound down for the winter, three railway workers came to the vicinity of Banff to prospect for minerals. While approaching Sulphur Mountain, William and Tom McCardell, and Frank McCabe chanced upon the outlets of several natural hot springs. The three men knew, in a land without plumbing a hot bath was worth a princely sum. They staked a claim and sought ownership of the springs, but were informed that since the mountains were not surveyed, no mineral claims could be allowed. Meanwhile, word of the springs got around, and others wanted in on the claim and the fortune it would surely bring.

Opposite: Banff Avenue, 1887.

Top: Banff Avenue, 1914.

The trio were inept in their business dealings regarding the springs. The hubbub created by various claims and counterclaims to "ownership" naturally attracted the attention of the federal government, which sent an agent to inspect the claim. Meanwhile, word of the springs also reached William Cornelius Van Horne, Vice President and

General Manager of the CPR He visited the springs now known as the Cave and Basin early in 1885, and with typical accuracy proclaimed: "These springs are worth a million dollars!"

Later that year, partly to settle the issue, but mostly at the prompting of the CPR., ownership of the springs passed from private dispute into government control. The federal government also desperately needed to recover moneys spent financing the railway. Quipping: "These springs will recuperate the patient and recoup the treasury", Prime Minister John A. Macdonald authorized the creation of the Banff Hot Springs Reserve in November 1885, forerunner of Canada's first national park.

Developments at the Cave and Basin began the following year. Bathers paid ten cents a swim. As the popularity of Banff grew with tourists from around the world, the facility was enlarged, but was still unable to meet the demand. Parks commissioner J.B. Harkin visited the site in 1911, and soon after, a complete redevelopment was proposed. Opened in 1914, the new $200,000 facility sported the largest swimming pool in the world at the time. This building saw use until its closure in 1976. It was reconstructed for the national parks centennial in 1985, and is now visited by more than one million people annually.

Top: One of the first bathhouses at the Cave and Basin, ca. 1888.

Opposite: Swimmers at the Cave and Basin, ca. 1910.

Top: Caretaker at the Cave
pool, Cave and Basin, ca. 1915.

Bottom: The re-developed Cave
and Basin in 1914.

Top: The swimming pool at the Cave and Basin, ca. 1914.

Bottom: Upper Hot Springs pool in winter, n.d.

The CPR experienced encouraging success with its railside stops at Glacier and Field during the summer of 1886. Visitors were in awe of the mountain scenery, and pleased to have comfortable services available in such remote settings. The railway desperately needed cash flow to help offset the debt incurred in its construction. CPR Vice-President and General Manager, William Cornelius Van Horne, took note of all this and hit upon an idea which would both help make the railway into a paying proposition, and create a

Opposite: The Banff Springs Hotel and the Bow River, ca. 1920.

Top: Tally-ho leaving the Banff Springs Hotel, ca. 1912.

tourism industry in mountainous western Canada. To Van Horne is attributed the statement: "Since we can't export the scenery, we'll have to import the tourists." With that aim in mind, in the fall of 1886 the CPR began construction of the pride of its mountain hotel fleet, the Banff Springs, at a site reportedly recommended by outfitter Tom Wilson, near the confluence of the Spray and Bow Rivers. The building would eventually cost a quarter of a million dollars.

In the summer of 1887, Van Horne visited the construction site and was shocked to see someone had oriented the plans backwards! The kitchen overlooked the rivers, and the guest rooms faced the forest. He hastily sketched addi-

tions to correct the matter. The 250 room hotel, complete with sulphur water piped from the Upper Hot Springs, opened June 1, 1888. It was the largest hotel in the world at the time. Room rates started at $3.50 a day.

The Banff Springs Hotel turned the tiny community of Banff into a destination resort. More than 5000 visitors arrived in the year after it opened. The hotel's nightly capacity was increased to 500 in 1903. During 1904, almost 10,000 guests registered, and many others were turned away to sleep in railway cars at the train station. The season was lengthened as needed to accommodate business. Van Horne's assessment had literally been right on the money.

Plans were drawn in 1911 to completely overhaul the building, but initially only one major expansion was undertaken – the 2 million dollar Painter Tower, completed in 1914. Between 1925 and 1928, the remainder of the expansion and reconstruction took place, yielding the main building we see today. Other additions were completed in 1990. The CPR lavished a great deal of money on furnishing the pride of its hotel fleet. Talented craftsmen worked with the finest materials. Windows were imported from Europe, and stone from Manitoba. The furniture and ornaments were painstakingly detailed to match period pieces. Much of the exterior of the building was eventually finished in "Rundle rock", quarried from the banks of the Spray River nearby.

Top: Interior of Banff Springs Hotel, ca. 1914.

Opposite top: View from the terrace of the Banff Springs Hotel, ca. 1940.

Opposite bottom: Courtyard of the Banff Springs Hotel, ca. 1912.

The Banff Springs was not the only hotel constructed in 1886. Dr. R.G. Brett, medical supervisor for the CPR, broke ground for his Sanitarium on the site now occupied by the park administration building. At this combination hotel/hospital, Dr. Brett treated patients with water piped from the Upper Hot Springs, and claimed miracle cures for a variety of ailments. Banff's fame spread rapidly, as a resort where health could be restored by clean mountain air and healing hot springs.

While development of the Cave and Basin Springs was carried out by the federal government, the Upper Hot Springs saw private enterprise. Dr. Brett also constructed his Grandview Villa adjacent to these springs in 1886. The restorative powers of the waters were attested to by abandoned crutches which lined the stairway from the Villa to the springs. In 1901, the Villa burned, and the government cancelled Brett's lease at the Upper Hot Springs and took over operations.

As with many frontier businessmen, Brett had his hand in many matters. He operated a transportation service, a drug store, and an opera house; sold bottled "Banff Lithia Water"; and became involved in politics. He served 13 years as a member of the provincial Legislative Assembly, and later was Lieutenant Governor of Alberta. His name is commemorated in Mt. Brett, in the Massive Range west of Banff.

Top: The grand opening of Dr. Brett's Grand View Villa Bathhouse, 1886. Dr. Brett is at the left on the lower landing. The stairway leads to the Upper Hot Springs.

Opposite top: Brett's Sanitarium, ca. 1890. The Sanitarium was a combination hotel and hospital which stood on the site now occupied by the Park administration building.

Opposite bottom: The dispensary at Brett's Sanitarium, ca. 1893.

Top: Canoes and steam
powered launch on the Bow
River, 1912.

Bottom: Corkscrew Drive on
Tunnel Mountain, with buggies
posed to illustrate, ca. 1920.

Top: A hive of activity - the C.P.R. station at Banff, ca. 1912.

Bottom: Horse and buggy meets horseless carriage. The Bow River bridge at Banff, a few years after the automobile was permitted in Rocky Mountains Park, ca. 1918.

The CPR initially took a distinctly rustic approach to development on the shores of Lake Louise, with construction of a simple log cabin in 1890. Access to Chalet Lake Louise, as it became known, was by foot or horseback from the railway siding called Laggan in the valley below. Visitors to the shores of Lake Louise in those early days were few, and included adventurous travellers who didn't mind roughing it. The Vaux family and Mary Schäffer, people who would later make important visits of exploration in the Rockies, were amongst them.

The original Chalet burned early in the summer of 1893. Those who visited Lake Louise that year camped on the lakeshore. The second Chalet was constructed in 1894, with an upper storey added the following year. Capacity was only a dozen guests, and the staff slept in tents and shacks nearby. In 1899, this Chalet was replaced by a much larger, Tudor-styled, timber and gable structure, designed by F.M. Rattenbury. Next, a 350 room concrete addition was erected in 1912. Finally, in 1916-17, a hydro-electric plant was built slightly downstream from the lake, bringing the latest of modern comforts to the sprawling building on the lakeshore.

Now capable of accommodating almost a thousand guests, the transformation from cabin to grand hotel was complete. The Chalet become known as the Chateau (pronounced "shah-TOE" – a French word which means "mansion"). Although still marketed by the CPR as a rustic destination, the Chateau, like the Banff Springs Hotel, was now able to deliver the services and atmosphere demanded by those accustomed to the finer things in life.

With the hotel's increased capacity, transferring guests between the railway station and the Chateau became a problem. Horse and buggy service could not keep up with the demand, and this means of conveyance was a constant source of complaint during poor weather. To rectify the problem the CPR began construction of a tramline in 1912. This gasoline powered mini-train on narrow-guage tracks could carry 180 passengers at a time. It made as many as 30 round trips a day until rendered obsolete by the automobile in 1930.

The wooden Rattenbury wing of the Chateau burned on July 3, 1924. Firefighting efforts saved the newer concrete wing. The Chateau remained open for the remainder of the summer, and construction of another addition soon commenced. Completed in May 1925, the new Chateau remained largely unchanged until the most recent renovations and reconstruction began in 1986.

Opposite: The first Chalet at Lake Louise, ca. 1890.

Opposite top: Chalet Lake Louise in 1894.

Opposite bottom: The much-expanded Chalet Lake Louise in 1909.

Above: View of Lake Louise from the porch of the Chalet, late 1890's.

Top: Chalet Lake Louise staff "hard times" dance in Hillside residence, 1912.

Bottom: Chateau Lake Louise ca. 1920, showing the concrete Painter wing, and the wooden Rattenbury wing.

Opposite top: Chalet Lake Louise from the rear, showing the Rattenbury wing and an open-air car on the tramline.

Opposite bottom: Car on the narrow-guage tramline, which operated between the Chalet and Lake Louise station from 1913-30.

Top: The Chateau under reconstruction, winter of 1924-25.

Left: Swiss Guides Ernest Feuz Jr. (left), and Rudolph Aemmer, manning a fire hose during the Chateau fire.

Opposite: The wooden Rattenbury wing of the Chateau in flames, July 3, 1924.

The view at Moraine Lake features an unrefined beauty, more challenging to the eye than the incredible symmetry of Lake Louise, the open vista of Bow Lake, or the tranquillity of the Vermilion Lakes. Here is a solemn and spectacular reminder of the physical origin of the Rockies: walls of ice-cleaved rock are thrust towards a dizzying sky, and mirrored in the perfect, watery jewel below.

Walter Wilcox and Samuel Allen were the first to glimpse Moraine Lake,

during their attempt on Mt. Temple in 1893. Allen gained a distant view of the lake again the following summer, naming it and the peaks in the surrounding valley with Stoney words representing the numerals one to ten. It is surprising the first recorded visit to the lake's shore was not until 1899. The visitor, Walter Wilcox, inadvertently began a debate amongst geologists. Assuming the lake was dammed by a pile of glacial rubble, Wilcox renamed it Moraine. The more popular theory today states the lake was dammed by a rockslide.

Until the Moraine Lake Road was roughed out a decade later, the journey to the lakeshore was an ambitious undertaking. With the advent of auto travel in the 1920's, the

Canadian Pacific Railway constructed an auto bungalow camp on the lakeshore, precursor of today's Moraine Lake Lodge.

Moraine Lake has been featured on the Canadian twenty dollar bill since 1969. Today only peaks nine and ten – Neptuak and Wenkchemna – bear Allen's original names. Peak six has been named for Allen, and the Ten Peaks, as they had become known, are now officially called the Wenkchemna Peaks.

Opposite top: Interior of Chateau Lake Louise, ca. 1930.

Opposite bottom: Reflecting ball on the front lawn of the Chateau, ca. 1920.

Top: Film crew for the movie *The Alaskan*, at Moraine Lake, 1924.

During the height of activity in and around Banff, the vicinity of Jasper was yet awaiting its heyday. The fur trade fell into decline in the 1850's, and with it ceased the twice annual passing of the voyageurs through the Athabasca Valley. The next period of visitation ended abruptly in 1881, when after almost a decade of survey-ors' toil, the CPR abandoned the Yellowhead Pass route. Thus, in the late 19th century the Jasper area was the wilderness domain of a few Natives, trappers and homesteaders. It would stay that way until after Canada's second transcontinental railway, the Grand Trunk Pacific, was proposed in 1902.

"Jasper" had been an employee of the Hudson's Bay Company, and for a time operated a fur trade supply depot in the Ath-abasca Valley. This structure became known as Jasper House, and the name Jasper was applied to the general area. Jasper House, probably the oldest existing building in the Rockies at the time, was destroyed by railway surveyors in 1910. They used its wood to fashion a raft with which to cross the Athabasca River.

In 1893, Lewis Swift, an American expatriate, became the first settler in the area which would later become Jasper National Park. He built a cabin east of the present town, beneath the cliffs of The Palisade. There he ranched cattle and traded with the local Natives. Before the coming of the railway, "Swift's Place" was a well known stopover for travellers in the Athabasca Valley. Swift offered accommodation and information, and operated a cable ferry across the Athabasca River.

Top: Jasper House, a Hudson's bay Company supply post in the Athabasca Valley east of Jasper, in 1872.

Opposite top: Swift's Place in 1909. Lewis Swift was one of the first settlers in the Athabasca Valley.

Opposite bottom: Construction of the Grand Trunk Pacific Railway through Yellowhead Pass in 1911.

With the advent of rail travel in the Jasper area, the federal government realized there existed potential to create another national park. In 1907 it established Jasper Forest Park, forerunner of Canada's seventh national park. The town of Jasper, originally called Fitzhugh, had its origins in 1911, as a divisional point on the Grand Trunk Pacific Railway. An array of tents and shacks called "Tent City" provided some of the original accommodation for workers and visitors alike.

It was not until 1922, when the Grand Trunk Pacific was amalgamated into the Canadian National Railway, that development of Jasper Park Lodge on the shores of Lac Beauvert began. A central building, claimed to be the world's largest log structure, replaced the Tent City. For $3.00/day, the guests slept in log cabins, and wined, dined and socialized in the main lodge. By 1925 they could partake in golf on an 18 hole course as well. Reflecting Jasper's increasing popularity with visitors, expansion took place in 1927-28. The new Lodge had a capacity of 425 guests. It burned on July 15, 1952, and was immediately replaced by the present structure, built at a cost of 3 million dollars.

Top: "Tent City", the earliest accommodation at Jasper, ca. 1911.

Opposite top: The bungalows at Jasper Park Lodge, ca. 1925.

Opposite bottom: The lounge at Jasper Park Lodge, ca. 1925.

THE BUNGALOWS. JASPER PARK LODGE.

THE LOUNGE. JASPER PARK LODGE.

THE HIGH FRONTIER

It was inevitable mountaineering would became popular in the Rockies. The Canadian Pacific Railway was constructed through some of the most spectacular and challenging mountain scenery in the world. Hundreds of mountains were in view from the rails; all unclimbed, most were also unnamed. Thousands more peaks lay hidden beyond. The Rockies and Selkirks were virtual blank maps, inviting mountaineers summitward, to etch their names on the snowy pages of history.

Glacier House, Mt. Stephen House and Chalet Lake Louise were comfortable lodgings on the doorsteps to adventure and fame. But even more crucial to the development of mountaineering in Canada than the new accessibility of the Rockies and Selkirks, was the timing of the completion of the CPR. By the 1870's almost all the major mountains in Europe had been ascended. Mountaineers were eager for new terrain which offered the opportunity for coveted "first ascents". Thus the eyes of the world's mountaineering elite turned to Canada. As it had done before with the hot springs and its hotels, the CPR capitalized on this interest to create successful industry in the Rockies.

The first significant mountaineering ascents from the railway were made by government surveyors in the 1880's. These included Mt. Stephen at Field, and Mt. Rundle at Banff. A few other explorers climbed the odd ridge, and occasionally reached lesser summits during this time, but the birth of recreational mountaineering in the Rockies dates to the summer of 1893, in the mountains near Lake Louise. Samuel Allen, a student from Yale, had visited the Rockies briefly in 1891 and stayed at the original Chalet Lake Louise. Two years later he returned with fellow student, Walter Wilcox, to make attempts on Mts. Victoria and Temple. Although unsuccessful, the experience whetted the novice mountaineers' appetites for alpine adventure, and for Wilcox, began an interest in the Rockies which would continue until his death in 1940.

In 1894, the Yale Lake Louise Club, now five strong, returned and made first ascents of Mts. Temple and Aberdeen, along with extensive explorations of surrounding valleys. Not content merely with conquering the heights, members of this group spent considerable time and energy mapping, photographing and documenting what they saw –

Opposite: Climbers on the summit of Mt. Resplendent, during the 1913 Alpine Club of Canada, Mount Robson camp.

a trait common to many early mountaineers in the Rockies.

The following year, members of Boston's Appalachian Mountain Club made the first ascent of Mt. Hector, just north of Lake Louise. In 1896 this club's focus turned to Mt. Lefroy. On the summit rocks, with the ascent almost assured, Phillip Abbot fell to his death. It was the first recorded fatality in North American mountaineering.

In 1897, Peter Sarbach, a Swiss mountain guide was brought to the Rockies to vindicate Abbot's death.

With little difficulty, Sarbach led a talented Anglo-American party to the summit of Mt. Lefroy. Two days later, Mt. Victoria, the mountain which forms the glaciated backdrop at Lake Louise, was ascended. The CPR made note of these and other mountaineering successes in 1897, and two years later began staffing its mountain hotels with Swiss Guides, thus assuring climbers of greater safety in their pursuit. Suddenly, mountaineering in the Rockies was an avocation to which almost anyone could aspire.

The CPR was aware mountaineers visiting the Rockies would communicate their exploits to fellow climbers through publications and lectures, thus attracting more business to the mountain hotels. In addition to importing the guides, the railway went out of its way to cater to climbers. It gave them use of hand cars to allow travel on the rails at unusual hours, and cut trails to make easier the approaches to some peaks. These special favours paid off handsomely. In their widely read accounts, the climbers extolled the

beauty and challenge of the Rockies to the world. Walter Wilcox's first book, "Camping in the Rockies", became an instant success when published in 1896, and went through numerous printings and editions.

It didn't take long for the interest of the mountaineering elite to shift from the peaks adjacent to the Canadian Pacific Railway, to the unknown ranges further north. At the heart of this interest was the mythic lure of Mts. Hooker and Brown, two mountains adjoining Athabasca Pass, which from observations recorded by explorer David Douglas in 1827, towered a mile higher than any other mountains known in the Rockies. Ultimately it was proven Hooker and Brown were mountains of less than average stature, but over a period of a decade, they inspired half a dozen expeditions into the north country. It was on one of these expeditions, in 1898, Scottish mountaineer J.N. Collie and party made the first recorded observation and exploration of Columbia Icefield.

Opposite: The Yale Lake Louise Club's camp in Paradise Valley near Lake Louise, 1894.

Above: Samuel Allen near Opabin Pass, 1894.

In the late 1880's the glaciers of the Rockies and Selkirks were at the maximum extent of their most significant recent advance. The Victoria Glacier, beyond Lake Louise, extended 1.2 kilometres closer to the lake than at present. Athabasca Glacier blocked the valley now occupied by the Icefields Parkway. Today glaciologists study the landscape for clues, attempting to decipher the past and present behaviour of glaciers. In some cases they are literally able to complete the picture by referring to remarkable photographs depicting the extent of glacial ice in the decades around the turn of the century. Many of these photographs were the skilled work of upper class Quakers from Philadelphia, the Vaux family (pronounced vox).

George Vaux Sr. and family, first visited the Rockies and Selkirks in 1887. During the next forty years, various family members made annual visits to the Canadian mountains, taking particular interest in glaciers, photography and botany. They recorded detailed accounts of their travels and observations, publishing papers and presenting lectures at home in Philadelphia. Amongst their most enduring contributions are stunning black and white landscape images of the Rockies and Selkirks, taken shortly after the completion of the railway.

Top: William Vaux Jr. (with camera), and George Vaux (third from left), with Swiss Guides and companions on Victoria Glacier, 1900.

Opposite top: Louise Creek and a view to Mt. Victoria, Lake Louise, 1900.

Opposite bottom: Ice cave at the terminus of Yoho Glacier, 1906.

Travel north from Lake Louise on expeditions at the turn of the century was no easy matter. Construction and operation of the railway had brought a scourge of forest fires to the region. What few trails existed were choked with burned timber. The early expeditions northwards literally cut their way through the valley bottoms, amidst clouds of smoke, mosquitoes and horse flies. There emerged a new character in the history of the Rockies, more than equal to this task – the trail guide.

Colourful characters with diverse backgrounds, many trail guides would become legends in the Rockies. All but a few got their start with Tom Wilson's company in Banff. To the trail guides fell the responsibilities of choosing and clearing the route, taking care of the horses and clients, and dealing with the host of complications which could befall a party on the trail. They built rafts to cross lakes and hunted game when provisions dwindled. At night, around the campfire, they regaled their clients with stories tall and true. Few of the trail guides actually climbed, but their work was not without danger. One of the greatest hazards in these early mountaineering expeditions lay not on the peaks, but in crossing the swollen glacial melt rivers in the valley bottoms.

Among the most successful guides were Bill Peyto, Jimmy Simpson, Donald "Curly" Phillips, and Jim Brewster. With the advent of the automobile in the 1920's, trail riding declined, and other business opportunities presented themselves. With the resourcefulness they had demonstrated on the trail, many of the guides became entrepreneurs, providing a variety of services. Jimmy Simpson built Num-ti-jah Lodge at Bow Lake. Curly Phillips became a talented skier, and established a boat concession at Maligne Lake. The boat house he built there in 1929 still stands. The guiding business begun by Jim and Bill Brewster at Banff, eventually became Brewster Transportation and Tours.

Opposite: Packtrain fording the Sunwapta River, National Geographic Columbia Icefield Expedition, 1924.

Above: Campfire smudge at Calumet Creek, A.C.C./ Smithsonian Mt. Robson Expedition, 1911. Smoke from smudges kept mosquitos and horseflies away.

The dapper figure of the Swiss Guide – pipe in mouth, alpenstock in hand, rope coiled over the shoulder, and fedora on top – is a strong image in the history of the Rockies. The first Swiss Guide came to Canada in 1897. Others followed two years later, and quickly proved their value to both mountaineers and the CPR.

Members of the Feuz family (pronounced foits) were amongst the most prominent and longest serving of the guides. Edward Feuz Jr. led clients on thousands of ascents, including 78 "firsts", during a forty-one year career in Canada.

For $5.00 a day, novice or expert alike could hire a Swiss Guide to lead them onto the heights. Much of the Swiss Guides' work involved repetitive ascents of the regular routes on Mts. Stephen, Victoria, Lefroy, Temple and Sir Donald. But often they participated in more adventurous journeys of exploration further afield, during which dozens of new ascents were made. Typical of these were the outings of mountaineers James Outram, J.N. Collie, J.W.A. Hickson and James Monroe Thorington.

At first, the Guides returned to their families in Switzerland each winter. Eventually most remained in Canada year-round, taking employment as caretakers of the railway hotels during the off-season. The cpr built a village for the Swiss Guides near Golden, bc, so their families might also move to Canada. Ed Feuz Jr., last of the original Swiss Guides died at Golden in 1981, at age 96.

Opposite: Swiss Guides at the 1907 Alpine Club of Canada camp in Paradise Valley.

Above: Swiss Guides returning from the first ascent of Mt. Collie, on the Wapta Icefield in what is now Yoho National Park, August 19, 1901. The dotted line marks their route to the summit.

Above: Swiss Guide Ed Feuz Jr.
leading a client on Saddleback
Mountain near Lake Louise, ca.
1910.

Opposite: Ed Feuz Jr. on the
upper Victoria Glacier in 1925.

At various times in the early and mid-1890's, the attention of mountaineers had been riveted on the yet unclimbed Mt. Lefroy near Lake Louise, and also on Mts. Hooker and Brown further north. South of Banff, the most desired peak was Mt. Assiniboine, popularly called "the Matterhorn of the Rockies".

Assiniboine is the sixth highest peak in the range. It is a landmark for hundreds of kilometres in the mountaineer's view from other summits. Various expeditions organized by Allen, Wilcox and others in the 1890's, had increased the knowledge of the mountain and its approaches, but had failed to ascend the peak.

In 1901, Edward Whymper, conqueror of the European Matterhorn and may other peaks in the Alps, convinced the CPR to sponsor him and a troupe of Swiss Guides in a summer of exploration in the Rockies. Whymper was to lend his stature to published accounts of the Rockies by authoring a few himself. He was also to make suggestions to the CPR concerning the establishment of facilities and the building of trails.

Opposite: Mt. Assiniboine, the "Matterhorn of the Rockies", 1899.

Above: James Hector (seated), with Edward Whymper, at Glacier House, 1903.

None too secretly it was hoped he would achieve a publicity coup by climbing the Canadian Matterhorn as well.

Being past his mountaineering prime, Whymper had no real interest in this objective. Other than a series of new, relatively easy ascents near Vermilion Pass and in Yoho, he accomplished little of note. In September 1901, Assiniboine was climbed by Whymper's companion of the summer, the Reverend James Outram. (pronounced OOT-rum). The ascent of Assiniboine was one of Outram's many mountaineering achievements in the summers of 1900-1902. He also made first ascents of Mt

Columbia on Columbia Icefield – the second highest mountain in the Rockies – and Mt. Bryce, one of the most difficult peaks in the range.

Whymper made visits to the Rockies in subsequent summers. In 1903 at Glacier House, he met Sir James Hector, then 69 years old. Hector had been geologist and doctor to the Palliser Expedition of 1857-60. During this expedition Hector travelled extensively in the Rockies, and amongst other accomplishments made the first crossing of Kicking Horse Pass. It is fortunate this meeting of two giants of exploration was recorded on film.

"Wild" Bill Peyto (pronounced PEE-toe) typified the eccentric characters attracted to the profession of trail guide. Not a native of the wild west, Peyto hailed from an unlikely place – Kent, England. Wanderlust brought him to Canada at age eighteen, and eventually to the mountains, where his surprising abilities as woodsman, hunter and prospector flourished. Peyto cultivated a self-taught knowledge of geology, and spent several years prospecting near Banff before joining Tom Wilson's company in 1893 or 1894.

Of Peyto, Walter Wilcox commented: "His forté was doing things, not talking about them." Wild Bill was guide on a number of important mountaineering expeditions, including those of J.N. Collie in 1897 and 1898, and Whymper and Outram in 1901. He was known as a man of contrasts: his quiet manners were offset by his wild garb and off-beat sense of humour. After a stint in the Boer War, Peyto set up his own guiding business. Later he served in the First World War, joining the park warden service in Banff upon his return.

The overlook at Bow Summit was a favourite haunt of Peyto's, during expeditions which camped in the vicinity of Bow Lake. Thus the waters in the spectacular view from the lookout became known as Peyto Lake.

Opposite: "Wild" Bill Peyto, trail guide and outfitter, 1895.

Above: Bill Peyto(left), Hugh Stutfield (foreground) and J.N. Collie at camp in the Mistaya Valley, during the 1898 expedition which discovered Columbia Icefield.

Jimmy Simpson cut his teeth in the trail business as camp cook working for Tom Wilson's company from 1897-1901. Simpson must have learned the ropes of trail life well, for from this humble beginning he emerged as perhaps the most knowledgeable and proficient trail guide ever to work in the Rockies. Known to Natives as Nashan-essen – which means "wolverine go quick" – Simpson had a remarkable ability to travel swiftly in the mountains. He was also a great hunter, and is credited with taking a world record bighorn ram in 1920. Simpson parleyed his skills into a successful hunting business, cultivating an elite and wealthy clientele from the eastern United States. In the winters he hunted and trapped alone in the country north of Bow Lake.

Simpson began building Num-ti-Jah Lodge (pronounced numm-TAH-zjaah) on the shores of Bow Lake in 1920, replacing a camp he had operated since the early 1900's. The octagonal shape of the main lodge resulted from the desire to build a large structure, when only short timbers were available.

Simpson spent many of his later days at Num-ti-Jah. As with many mountain men and women, he was long-lived. He died in 1972 at age 95. The mountain immediately north of the lake was named in his honour the following year.

Above: Teepee at Bow Lake, Columbia Icefield Expedition, 1924.

Opposite bottom: Jimmy Simpson, legendary trail guide and builder of Num-ti-Jah Lodge.

During a 1923 expedition to Columbia Icefield, trail guide Jimmy Simpson did something he'd been wanting to try for years – he drove his pack horses along the icy surface of Saskatchewan Glacier. Simpson's motivation was a shortcut on the journey between Castleguard Meadows, on the southern edge of Columbia Icefield, and Sunwapta Pass. The horses apparently took to the ice with little fuss, which is surprising, given the temperament of the average pack animal. Little did Simpson realize, he had started a trend.

The following year, during the National Geographic expedition to Columbia Icefield, horses were again taken onto Saskatchewan Glacier. Photographer Byron Harmon got great mileage out of the unlikely image of a packtrain on ice. Castleguard Meadows soon became a regular stopping place on trail rides between Jasper and Lake Louise, organized by Jack Brewster. The meadows were routinely reached by crossing the ice, and the excursion became known as "The Glacier Trail."

Above: Packtrain on Saskatchewan Glacier, Columbia Icefield Expedition, 1924.

Opposite top: "The Glacier Belle" on Glacier Lake, 1902. J.N. Collie's mountaineering party used the raft to cross the lake on their way to the Lyell Icefield.

Opposite bottom: Ice cave at the terminus of Athabasca Glacier, 1914.

When the Vaux family visited the Canadian mountains in 1889, they brought with them a 28 year old companion from Philadelphia, Mary Sharples. During a stop at Glacier House, Mary was introduced to Dr. Charles Schäffer, whom she married soon after returning home.

Beginning in 1891, the Schäffers made annual journeys to the Rockies, for the purpose of collecting and cataloguing botanical specimens. With consider-

able skill, Mary rendered illustrations for the collection. When her husband died in 1903, she decided to complete the botanical study, looking further afield for specimens than on previous travels. More accustomed to carriage and parlour than horseback and camp, Mary sought to toughen herself for life on the trail and approached Tom Wilson for assistance. Wilson put at her disposal guide Billy Warren, who would shepherd Mary for almost thirty years. The two eventually married in 1915.

With her work on the botanical collection completed in 1905, Mary's sole reason for taking to the trails was now the joy of exploration. In particular, she was lured by the rumoured existence of a large lake in the north country; the lake known today as Maligne. An expedition in 1907 failed to reach the lake, but took Mary to the remote north edge of Columbia Icefield. In 1908, using a crude map drawn by Stoney chief Sampson Beaver, Mary and party reached Maligne Lake from the south, and spent

several days on a raft exploring the largest body of water in the Rockies. Mary published a popular account of these journeys in 1911. *Old Indian Trails* was well received and made her into a celebrity. At 50 years of age, Mary then gave up trail life to reside at Banff, where she lived until her death in 1939.

Above: Chief Sampson Beaver and family, 1907. Sampson provided Mary Schäffer with a crude map of the route to Maligne Lake.

Right: Mary Schäffer, who explored Maligne Lake in 1908.

Arthur Oliver (A.O.) Wheeler was an Irish-born, land surveyor, trained in the use of photography for map making. As with the other topographic surveyors who preceded him in the Rockies and Selkirks, his work typically involved occupying survey stations on mountain tops. As a consequence, Wheeler developed the skills of a mountaineer. In 1901, he began to advocate the formation of a Canadian mountaineering club, to promote climbing, study, and appreciation of the mountains of western Canada.

In February 1906, Wheeler presented the idea for founding the Alpine Club of Canada to an executive meeting of the Canadian Pacific Railway at Field. The railway realized the tourism benefits which would accrue from the association, and whole-heartedly supported the idea. For the next two decades, the CPR provided assistance in staging annual mountaineering camps, and the attending mountaineers published widely read accounts of their exploits, thus attracting more visitors to the Rockies.

In 1911, Wheeler led an expedition to the vicinity of Mt. Robson. Largely as a result of the expedition report, Mt. Robson Provincial Park was established two years later, protecting the area around the highest mountain in the Rockies. From 1913-25, Wheeler took part in the British Columbia/Alberta, Interprovincial Boundary Survey, during which he named many features in the Rockies.

Above left: A.O. Wheeler, surveyor, mountaineer and founder of the Alpine Club of Canada, 1944 or 1945.

Above right: A.O. Wheeler operating a survey camera during the Interprovincial Boundary Survey, which delineated the Alberta/B.C border between 1913 and 1925.

Opposite top: Members of the Alpine Club of Canada near Yoho Glacier, 1914.

Opposite bottom: Members of the Alpine Club of Canada at the Giant Steps, Paradise Valley, 1907.

With an elevation of 3954m/ 12972ft, Mt. Robson is the highest mountain in the Canadian Rockies, standing head and shoulders above the rest. Before the construction of the Grand Trunk Pacific Railway through the area in 1911, the mountain and its environs were known only to trappers, prospectors and a few intrepid explorers and guides. The first mountaineering attempts on Robson took place in 1908. The following year, Reverend George Kinney and trail guide Donald "Curly" Phillips made a series of

Opposite: The east face of Mt. Robson, 1913.

Above: Climbers with movie camera on Mt. Resplendent, 1918. Mt. Robson is in the background.

bold and ill-equipped attempts on the imposing west face of the mountain. On the last of these Kinney claimed success, although it later became apparent they had not quite reached the summit.

Conquest of the mountain then became a principal aim of the Alpine Club of Canada. During the 1911 Smithsonian/ACC expedition to Mt. Robson, Club President A.O. Wheeler scouted the vicinity as a location for an ACC camp. Wheeler wanted the highest peak in the Rockies to be climbed by Canadians. From the 1913 camp at Robson Pass, Austrian born mountain guide Conrad Kain, led two ACC members to the summit, fulfilling Wheeler's desire. Robson was one of fifty "first

ascents" Kain made during 25 seasons of guiding in Canada.

Many climbing routes have since been established on Robson, and this difficult mountain has lost none of its appeal to mountaineers.

Above: Conrad Kain, the
Austrian mountain guide who
led the first ascent of Mt.
Robson in 1913.

Opposite: A.C.C. members
inspecting a crevasse on Robson
Glacier, 1913.

PROFESSIONS AND PASTIMES

Ever since the wife of Prime Minister John A. Macdonald rode on the cowcatcher of a train from Lake Louise to Vancouver in the summer of 1886, the Rockies have seen an array of professions and pastimes – everything from basic industry to madcap novelty.

In Banff's transition from frontier town to tourism centre, the pluck and perseverance of the early surveyors, prospectors, loggers and railway builders, quickly gave way to the savvy of the main street businessman. While most industrial enterprise in the Rockies faded into history, curtailed by economics, or prohibited by park regulations, tourism flourished. It is not surprising the most successful businessmen placed the tourist trade foremost amongst their diverse interests. Those who rose to the top in Banff – Dr. R.G. Brett, Jim Brewster and Norman Luxton – all owned hotels.

Luxton also founded the newspaper, *The Banff Crag and Canyon,* and was a key figure in two of Banff's oldest traditions: Banff Indian Days, and the Banff Winter Carnival. The Indian Days, during which Stoney Natives came to Banff to entertain hotel guests, reportedly originated in 1889 when the CPR mainline flooded, stranding hundreds of idle patrons at the Banff Springs. The celebration of Native culture was held annually until 1978, and for many epitomized the mix of "wild west" and mountains, central to the lure of the Rockies. Up until the first Winter Carnival in 1917, Banff had been a destination offering services in summer only. The carnival was a gimmick in an ultimately successful attempt to create winter business in Banff. The late 1920's saw the beginning of another annual event, the Highland Gathering at the Banff Springs Hotel. This celebration of traditional Scottish culture, became a popular, if somewhat contrived, summertime event.

The Rockies' reputation for spectacular scenery allowed several photographers to create prosperous businesses in postcards and movies, bringing views of the mountains to the world. Most successful was Byron Harmon, who arrived in Banff in 1903. Harmon is literally our principal visual witness of Rockies' history. He was named official photographer to the Alpine Club of Canada at its outset in 1906. By

Opposite: Elliott Barnes demonstrating his camera to a Stoney Native at Kootenay Plains, 1907.

his participation on many mountaineering ascents, Harmon's photography offered a unique and remarkably popular perspective on the Rockies. Many of the photographs reproduced in this book come from the collection of more than 6500 Byron Harmon images, now preserved in the Whyte Museum at Banff.

The advent of the automobile during the second decade of the 19th century, made business in the Rockies mercurial. Some traditional enterprises, such as trail guiding, declined, as North Americans expressed their new found fascination with the horseless carriage. Ultimately of course, the automobile created more industry in tourism than it undermined, and some

guides and outfitters capitalized on new opportunities – operating lodges, boat tours, and pioneering downhill skiing in the Rockies.

Before the days of refrigeration, the ice harvest was an important annual enterprise in the Rockies. Large chunks of ice were cut from the frozen surface of Lake Louise and the Bow River, and stored in ice houses for use in stores and hotels the following summer. This difficult job provided employment for Swiss Guides and outfitters during the off-season.

Probably the strangest endeavour in the history of the Rockies took place in the winter of 1943, at Patricia Lake near Jasper. Desperate for a vessel which would be invincible to

attack by German U-boats, the Allies experimented with making an aircraft carrier from a mixture of ice and wood chips. Despite enthusiastic backing by none other than Sir Winston Churchill, the bizarre idea was fraught with problems, and was abandoned the following winter.

Above: Banff Avenue during the Winter Carnival, 1929.

opposite top: The ice palace at the first Winter Carnival, 1917. Prisoner of war labour was used to construct the palace.

Opposite bottom: Photographer Byron Harmon on Castleguard Mountain, 1924.

ICE PALACE BANFF AT NIGHT.

335 CINNAMON BEAR.

Most visitors to Banff at the turn of the century had a peculiar need to obtain a wilderness experience without straying from the lap of luxury. The essence of this experience was the opportunity to view wild animals. Ever willing to cater to tourists' needs, the federal government constructed a nature museum at Banff in 1895, at which stuffed examples of wildlife were displayed. In 1904, a zoo and aviary were added on the museum grounds. As it little mattered to the visitors that the animals were captive and not wild, neither did it matter the zoo included wildlife not native to the Rockies. One of the most popular animals was a polar bear! Reflecting a more contemporary outlook on wildlife, the zoo was removed in 1937.

The Banff Buffalo Paddock originated in 1897, when Plains bison were donated to the park. The last record of a free-roaming bison (buffalo) in the Rockies was 1858. A century earlier, it is estimated 30- 60 million of these animals had ranged through central and western North America. One of the bison reintroduced to Banff, nicknamed "Sir Donald" after its donor, was thought to be the oldest existing range-born bison at the time. Sir Donald was 38 years old when he died. Eventually, an array of other animals was kept at the Buffalo Paddock. Today, only bison remain.

Opposite: Zookeeper feeding a cinnamon bear at the Banff zoo, n.d.

Above: "Sir Donald", one of the original bison at the Banff Buffalo Paddock, 1906.

Top: Mountain goats at the buffalo paddock, n.d.

Bottom: Animal heads and pelts at the "Sign of the Goat" curio store, Banff, ca. 1906.

Opposite: The family of photographer Elliott Barnes, picnicking on Stoney Squaw mountain near Banff, 1907 or 1908.

A visit to Lake Minnewanka and the Tunnel Mountain Hoodoos has long been one of the most popular side trips at Banff. Nicknamed "Devil's Lake", after a Native legend which tells of a malevolent creature in its waters, Minnewanka is in truth today a reservoir. First dammed in 1912 to provide hydro-electricity for Banff, subsequent damming projects have created the largest body of water in Banff National Park, raising the original water level 25 metres, and extending its length from 16 to 24 kilometres. A village which formerly occupied the lakeshore is now submerged.

Boat tours have operated on Minnewanka since the 1880's, and for a time around the turn of the century, ice boating in winter was extremely popular.

Coal was discovered in the vicinity of Lake Minnewanka in 1885. The Canadian Pacific Railway developed a claim on the slopes of Cascade Mountain in 1903, to mine coal to fire its locomotives. Eventually, fifty-five kilometres of tunnels were excavated. When production peaked in 1911, 300 men were employed below ground, and 180 above. More than 1000 people lived in the town named Bankhead, which flourished nearby.

Labour unrest and poor economics put end to the mining in 1922, and soon after, every building in Bankhead was removed or demolished. Many were transported to Banff, Canmore and Calgary. The miners either took up a new way of life locally, or moved on to other coal mining areas in western North America.

Top: Tour boats, the *Daughter of the Peaks* and *The Aylmer*, Lake Minnewanka, 1910.

Opposite top: The tipple, where coal was sorted at the mining town of Bankhead, ca. 1906.

Opposite bottom: Miners at Bankhead, ca. 1915.

Top: Ice boating on Lake Minnewanka, 1908.

Bottom: Ice harvest on the Bow River near Canmore, winter of 1921-22. The ice was used by stores and hotels for refrigeration.

Opposite: Log run on the Bow River above Bow Falls, ca. 1890. Timber berths and mining claims were permitted in the mountain national parks until 1930.

Opposite: Stoney Natives at Banff Indian Days, n.d.

Above: Teepee at Maligne Lake, 1924.

Left.:Stoney Natives racing horses in the foothills near Morley, 1907.

Above: Yoho park warden Jack
Giddie with horse on Mt.
Burgess, ca. 1930.

Opposite: Horses on Victoria
Glacier, 1922. Horses were used
to pack supplies partway along
the ice during construction of
Abbot Pass Hut.

Opposite: The tea house at Lake Agnes, 1923. The tea house was reconstructed in 1981.

Top: Looking out at the Bow River from Hole-in-the-Wall, a cave high on Mt. Cory, n.d.

Bottom: Tom Wilson and George Fear at their Banff Avenue curio store, ca. 1894.

The Banff Park Museum, near the Bow River on Banff Avenue, is the oldest natural history museum in western Canada. Norman Sanson was its curator from 1896-1942. The museum benefited greatly from Sanson's dedicated work. His duties included the collection of plant and animal specimens for the museum, and the recording of weather data from the observatory atop Sulphur Mountain. In all he made over 1000 trips to the observatory, (without benefit of a gondola), and hiked over 32,000 kilometres in the line of his work. Sanson's last trip to the top of Sulphur was in 1945, to make observations of a solar eclipse.

Sanson contributed over one half of the specimens on display in the Banff Park Museum. Under his administration, it became known as "The University of the Hills." The Museum was proclaimed a National Historic Site in 1985. The ruins of the observatory are on a summit of Sulphur Mountain now known as Sanson Peak.

Opposite: Upper Falls in Johnston Canyon, n.d.

Above: Norman Sanson (front row, left) and friends at the observatory on Sulphur mountain, during Sanson's 1000th ascent, July 1, 1931.

Opposite: Scene from the
movie, *The Silent Force,* filmed
at Lake Louise, ca. 1925.

Above: Chief John Hunter on
the Mt. Norquay chairlift, ca.
1950.

While there had been a lack of human activity in the Jasper area in the quarter century following completion of the Canadian Pacific Railway to the south, industry and enterprise came quickly to the north country with the establishment of Jasper Forest Park, and the construction of the Grand Trunk Pacific Railway. One of the most prominent industries had its origin in the discovery of coal on the slopes of Roche Miette in 1908. Two years later, Jasper Park Collieries began mining the claim. Production peaked in 1912 and the town of Pocahontas, named after the noted mining centre in Virginia, sprang up on the banks of the Athabasca River. Soon after, failing economics, strikes and accidents began to plague the mine. It closed in 1921.

Miners from Pocahontas roughed out a track to Miette Hot Springs, the Rockies' hottest, in 1910, and built the first bathhouse there in 1913. During a strike in 1919 they constructed a hot pool. The federal government oversaw construction of the 18 kilometre Miette Hot Springs road in 1933, as a Depression make-work project. Full development of the springs took place in 1937.

Mt. Edith Cavell has long been one of the most popular sightseeing destinations in the Jasper area. The mountain was named in 1915 to commemorate nurse Edith Cavell, executed for assisting the escape of Allied prisoners of war. It was first climbed the same year. The road to the base of the mountain was completed in 1924, and a tea house operated nearby from 1929 to 1972.

Above: The coal mine at Pocahontas, some time between 1910 and 1921.

Opposite top: Early developments at Miette Hot Springs, ca. 1920. Miners from Pocahontas built these structures.

Opposite bottom: Climbers on the summit cornice of Mt. Edith Cavell, 1943.

Much to the chagrin of the old-guard trail guides, who preferred winter travel on snowshoes, skiing in the Rockies began to catch on in the 1920's. Jimmy Simpson called skiers: "people with wooden heads and feet to match." Nonetheless, the Banff Ski Club was founded, and its members took their skill and enthusiasm to the slopes of Mt. Norquay, above the town. Soon after, northeast of Lake Louise in the Skoki Valley (pronounced SKOWE-key), ski enthusiasts constructed the first back country ski lodge in the Rockies. Now a rich part of the area's human history, Skoki Lodge celebrated its 60th anniversary in 1991.

In 1934, Jim Brewster obtained the winter lease on a CPR trail cabin just below the Sunshine Meadows. The area had been visited by skiers from Banff during several previous winters, and was noted for its delightful skiing conditions. Brewster explored the area's potential as a ski resort for two seasons. Results were promising, and the cabin was bought outright. Mountain guides were soon hired to teach skiing to guests. The Sunshine ski area was born.

In the early days, before rope tows, lifts and snowmobiles, downhill skiers earned their runs by attaching traction-giving seal skins to their skis, and "skinning" up hill. The first permanent lift at Sunshine was installed in 1945. Access to some of the upper ski slopes was provided by snowmobile buses, and in the days before the gondola, the ski area was reached by a hair-raising drive along the access road from Healy Creek.

Above: Ski jumping at Mt. Norquay, n.d.

Opposite: Sunshine Lodge and snowmobile bus, n.d.

Top: Ike Mills and dog team on Ptarmigan Lake, packing supplies to Skoki Lodge, 1932.

Bottom: A skier ascending a slope at Sunshine, in the days before rope tows and chairlifts, ca. 1938.

Top: Skiers demonstrating the style of the day near Skoki, 1932.

Bottom: Skoki Lodge, first backcountry ski lodge in the Rockies. The original building opened in the winter of 1931. Construction of this addition took place in 1936.

WONDER ROADS

The advent of the automobile ushered in a new era in Rockies' tourism, and challenged the CPR's twenty-five year old dominance. However, changes did not happen overnight. The horseless carriage initially received the cold shoulder in the national parks. Reflecting the misgivings with which the first automobiles were viewed, the federal government enacted restrictions, effectively banning them. In the Rockies, the matter was somewhat academic during the early 1900's, since the greatest restriction to auto travel was the absence of a road to Banff!

The first road into the park was constructed in 1909, but autos which arrived at the park gate were denied access until two years later, when they could proceed as far as Banff townsite. Regulations governing auto use were gradually relaxed, and by June, 1915, most of the former carriage roads around the townsite were opened to motor vehicles. Sensing the potential for greater visitation, explorers, park administrators, and businessmen alike were soon predicting and advocating the construction of roads, to make the wonders of the Rockies accessible to all.

Points beyond Banff remained the realm of the railway and pack horse until construction of the road to Lake Louise commenced in 1914. Completed in 1920, this project employed prisoners of war, internees and conscientious objectors. Today, the Bow Valley Parkway follows the route they cleared. A proposal to link Banff and Windermere by highway in 1910, resulted in the creation ten years later of Kootenay, Canada's tenth national park. When private interests were unable to complete the road, the federal government took over the project, in return for British Columbia ceding title to land adjacent to the highway. Banff, Yoho, Glacier and Jasper had been "railway parks". Kootenay was Canada's first "highway park".

With inroads literally being made into its mountain domain, the CPR could read the writing on the wall. Rather than opposing the burgeoning trend towards automobile travel, the railway once again demonstrated its business sense, and jumped on the bandwagon. In the 1920's, it began construction of auto "bungalow camps" at various locations in the Rockies. Some of these camps evolved into commercial accommodations which still operate today. Storm Mountain and Moraine Lake Lodges are examples.

Opposite: Truck transporting a canoe through Sinclair Canyon in Kootenay National Park, 1923.

The federal government also perceived the automobile as central to the future of tourism in the Rockies, and opened numerous roadside campgrounds. The perception proved accurate. The automobile's dominance has lasted more than 70 years.

In 1926, "The Kicking Horse Trail" was completed through Yoho, utilizing abandoned railway grades on the Big Hill above Field. This roadbed would eventually become part of the Trans-Canada Highway, the longest paved road in the world. The section through the Rockies opened in 1958. Although die-hard motorists had for decades been making the bone-jarring trip along railway grades either side of Yellow-head Pass, the Yellowhead Highway was finally completed through Jasper National Park in 1968.

The first complete journey by trail from Banff to Jasper along the present day route of the Icefields Parkway was made in 1904, by a hunting party outfitted by Jim Brewster. Professor A.P. Coleman, an old hand at exploration of the Rockies, made a similar trip three years later, and became an enthusiastic supporter of a developed road linking Lake Louise and Jasper – a route he called "The Wonder Trail." Coleman would live to see this idea become reality. He traveled south from Jasper on the partially completed road in 1936.

Construction of the Icefields Parkway commenced in 1931, as a make-work project during the Great Depression. Crews worked towards each other from Jasper and Lake Louise, meeting at the Big Bend near Columbia Icefield in 1939. With very

little in the way of heavy equipment to aid their task, workers toiled for $5.00 per month plus room and board. Horses brought in from the prairies to assist in the clearing operations were noticed to suffer with the effects of altitude at Bow Pass, the highest point crossed by roadway in Canada. Many of the construction camps used by the workers became the sites of today's roadside camp-grounds.

The finished product was a 230 kilometre gravel road, 6.5 metres in width, and in no place steeper than 8%.

Much of the original grade is still in use today. The Icefields Parkway was officially opened in 1940, and the scenery it offered the motorist was heralded as "twenty Switzerlands in one." The road was up-graded and paved between 1956 and 1961, and is still considered by many to be the most spectacular drive in the world.

In 1990 the Icefields Parkway celebrated its 50th anniversary, and Jasper National Park hosted a reunion of some of those who had worked on the original construction.

Opposite: The entrance to Rocky Mountains Park (Banff), 1921.

Above: The Bow River and mountains near Lake Louise, from the Banff-Lake Louise Road, now the Bow Valley Parkway, 1921.

Top: Tunnel through avalanche debris on the Yoho Valley Road, ca. 1930. The photo was taken in early summer.

Bottom: Car at Lake Minnewanka, ca. 1920.

Opposite: A Brewster tour bus at Takakkaw Falls in the early 1930's.

Top: Radium Hot Springs, early 1920's.

Bottom: Workers using hand tools to clear the grade for the Icefields Parkway, ca. 1932.

Opposite: Sightseeing cars on the Vermilion Lakes Road, 1924.

COLUMBIA ICE FIELDS
BANFF-JASPER. HIGHWAY.

Opposite top: The Columbia Icefield Chalet and Athabasca Glacier, early 1940's.

Above: Snowmobile bus on Athabasca Glacier, early 1950's.

Left: Brewster tour buses at the terminus of Athabasca Glacier, early 1950's.

Top: Campers at an unidentified roadside campground during the 1920's.

Bottom: Moraine Lake and buildings of the "bungalow camp", ca. 1928.

Opposite: Brewster sightseeing bus at Crowfoot Glacier viewpoint, late 1950's.

Photography Credits

The author is particularly grateful to the staff of the Archives, Whyte Museum of the Canadian Rockies, for their assistance with this project.

In the photograph captions, "n.d." means no specific date can be matched to the photograph; "ca." means "circa", or approximately.

Whyte Museum of the Canadian Rockies, Banff
A.B. Thom: 14, 24
A.L. Mumm: 39 upper
Bert Prendergast: 80 lower
Bill Gibbons: 91
Boorne and May: 9 lower, 10
Brewster Transport collection: 103, 106-107, 109
Bruno Engler: 95
Byron Harmon collection : front cover, 4, 12, 17, 18 both, 19 upper, 20, 22, 23 upper, 26 lower, 27 upper, 32 both, 39 lower, 42, 48, 49, 50, 51 upper, 58-59, 60, 61 lower, 65 both, 66, 67, 68, 69, 72, 73 upper, 74, 76 upper, 82 upper, 83 upper, 86, 87 upper, 88, 94, 96 upper, 97 upper, 98, 100, 101, 102 both, 105, 108 lower, 11l
Coast Publishing: 15
Ed Feuz Jr. collection: 34 lower
Edward Whymper: 51
Elliott Barnes: 75, 76 lower, 77, 79 upper, 80 upper, 82-83 lower
F.H. Slark: 41 both
G. Morris Taylor: 93 lower
George Noble: 21, 23 lower
George Paris: 25 lower
H. Woolley: 57
John Woodruff: 81
Lewis Freeman: 73 lower
Lloyd Harmon: 96 lower
Mary Schäffer collection: 55, 59 lower, 62-63, 70
Mollie Adams: 63 lower
Nicholas Morant: 107 upper
Peter and Catherine Whyte collection: 36 lower

Photographer unknown: 2, 7 upper, 19 lower, 27 lower, 35, 37, 52, 61 upper, 64 left, 78, 87 lower, 79, 89, 90, 97, 106 upper, rear cover
S.A. Smyth: 25 upper
S.S. Thompson: 16
Stedman Brothers: 26 upper
Underwood and Underwood: 108 upper
Vaux Family collection: 30 lower, 46, 47 both
W.J. Oliver: 84
Walter Wilcox: 44, 45, 53, 54, 56, 85

Glenbow-Alberta Institute, Calgary
Charles Horetzky: 38
Edgar Spurgeon: 40
Photographer unknown: 6, 7 lower, 8, 11 both, 28, 92, 93 upper, 104 upper

Provincial Archives of Alberta, Edmonton
Photographer unknown: 64 right

Jasper/Yellowhead Historical Society, Jasper
Photographer unknown: 104 lower

Canadian Pacific Corporate Archives, Montreal
O.B. Buell: 9 upper
Photographer unknown: 1, 13, 31, 33 both, 34 upper, 36 upper
R.H. Trueman: 30 upper

Author photo: Marnie Pole

Above: Terrace pool at the
Chateau, ca. 1925. Today the
terrace is used as an outdoor
restaurant during summer.

Graeme Pole

When mountaineer Graeme Pole first came to the Rockies in 1982, he was captivated by the exploits of climbers at the turn of the century. Research into the history of mountaineering added an interesting dimension to Graeme's own mountain travels, and served as a catalyst for studying other elements of the history of the mountain national parks.

Graeme lives in Field, BC, with his wife Marnie. He is a photographer, licensed independent interpretive guide, nordic ski instructor, and part-time employee of the British Columbia Ambulance Service. He is also the author of *Canadian Rockies* and *Walks and Easy Hikes in the Canadian Rockies* in the Altitude *SuperGuide* series.